HOW TO SUCK AT NETWORK MARKETING AND STILL DO RATHER WELL

CAROL STEVENSON

Who am I?

The rest of this book took me all of three weeks to write. This part took me forever. Who the heck am I?

My name is Carol Stevenson and I've been a network marketer since 2016. I consider myself to be a modern-day slasher (of the non-murdering kind, although on bad days I do come close to that). I am currently a wife/mum/bookkeeper/PTA treasurer/network marketer. In the past, I have been an events director/finance marketer/administrator/actress/professional English language speaker (yes that really is a job). So, you see, I like to slash a lot. It makes me great at dinner parties.

I have lived through six different careers, two life-changing illnesses, starting a family, fifteen house moves, and one marriage which is somehow still going strong even though my husband barely gets any attention from me. I live in beautiful rural Leicestershire with my family and the world's laziest dog, and thankfully I have no further plans to move again.

I enjoy brisk walking on cold sunny days, swimming and team sports, pub lunches before the rugby, and very occasionally I manage a visit back to my favourite old haunt, the theatre. I love nothing more than to curl up with a book. This one should be read with a cup of tea and the good biscuits.

Praise for *How to suck at network marketing (and still do rather well)*

"This will definitely resonate with the partner on the street."

"This book really inspired a team member we shared it with. He hit top of the leaderboard for recruiting!"

"A great help to those who have just started and feel like they haven't managed to get any traction and an affirmation for those doing it their way that doing it their way is fine."

"This book is bloody amazing – no words really! I love the honesty, the real-life take on what it means to be a network marketer. And I could have almost written it myself, it's so me and probably millions of others out there, too. Great to know we're not all expected to be power hungry 'climb to the top of the tree in two minutes' kind of people because that's the impression that's given out generally. But wow, just wow, thank you so much for sharing."

"Have to say well done – a great way to summarise it. Personal but gives a great message."

"Love it and it definitely resonates with me."

"Great tips for us 'normal' distributors."

Contents

This book isn't for you... is it?

Hello, I'm Carol Stevenson. I have been a network marketer for seven years and I'm still only on the bottom few rungs of the ladder.

You're probably thinking, "Wait, what? I was told I could be earning millions after a few years in network marketing. I've been conned! Why am I even reading this?"

If that is indeed what went through your mind, there are two conclusions I might draw about you: 1) You are very believing – good on you; 2) You are indeed reading the wrong book.

That's because this book is NOT for people who are dreaming about a life of luxury on the beach. Network Marketing books (I should know, I've read them all) tend to be written by the leaders of the pack, the go-getters, the early adopters, who are earning millions after just 10 years in the business. "Look at me! And you can do this, too!" And that's fine if a life on the beach IS your goal. But it actually isn't mine and never has been.

Let me tell you a bit about where I come from in all this. I started my work within network marketing because I needed another £500 a month to break even. I had no designs to be top of the tree, no dream of living my life in luxury. I wasn't particularly excited about starting a new business either, I just thought it was worth a try; I had zero expectations, either of myself or of the company.

If anything, I was very *anti*-network marketing, I wanted nothing to do with the idea of "growing my team"; I just wanted to earn a second income without it taking up too much of my time. *That* was my goal, *not* to be rich.

And I strongly believe that being rich isn't the goal for most people. For most people, we start out in network marketing with a small seed of an idea that it could be a potential Plan B or a second income that gives us the change in our lives that we seek, whether that is a bit more money to keep the wolves from the door or a bit more time that we can spend with our loved ones. Most people's goal isn't to achieve the highest level of stardom in their business. When you think about it, that's the same for "normal" day jobs, too. Most people don't start a job on the check-out at Sainsbury's expecting or hoping to be promoted to CEO in 10 years' time. In fact, for many of us, that role sounds hideous; just think of the stress!* No, we work because we want to *live*, we want to *provide* for ourselves or our families, and we want nothing more than to find *balance* and hopefully a bit of *happiness*.

Too many of us, *way* too many in fact, start a network marketing business but then drop it straight away. We let our fears get the better of us, and we tell ourselves that (for whatever reason) we shouldn't do it. I find that such a huge shame, because the reason you signed up, the reason you gave up your hard-earned cash to join, was not to quit immediately. You have something in your life (or maybe a lack of something) that makes you want to make a change, and you saw that glimmer of possibility through network marketing. But something has put you off, whether that's a lack of faith in the company itself or (as often happens) a lack of confidence in yourself.

So, if you are thinking of quitting – or telling yourself that you're just going to put the business down for a while, that you'll get back to it – read this book. Dare I say it, lots of the other personal development books on network marketing are written by seriously motivated and successful people who can't relate to your life (at least, as it is right now). Call me a tortoise, but I can.** I've had my ups and downs – I've loved the business, I've hated it, I've gone at it full-tilt, I've plodded along. Yet, somehow I'm still here, I'm achieving my goals with interest and now I'm having fun with it.

Here's how you can, too – on *your* terms.

*Apologies to the CEO of Sainsbury's if you are reading this. I really hope you love your job.

**During the Queen's funeral on TV, the Archbishop told the audience to "do as the Saviour taught us". My young daughter misheard, turned to look at me quizzically and asked, "What's a Saviour Tortoise?" We all simply collapsed. I love the notion of a Saviour Tortoise, so he comes up quite a bit on the next few pages.

Don't trust network marketing? Join the club!

Let's get one thing straight, right from the start.

It's OK to dislike network marketing.

There, I've said it. Because I do, I hate it – and I've been in the business of network marketing for many years now. The words alone make me want to vomit.

It's an ingrained reaction that I simply can't control. It started when I was about five. I have a vague memory of my mum coming home from a party with friends. She was probably a little bit tiddly (forgive me, Mum, but I reckon you might have been), and she was ranting about how she'd really looked forward to the party but it had turned out to be a networking party and she had felt like she was being sold to the entire time. That was the first time I heard the term "network marketing", and I learnt that it was A Bad Thing.

Fast forward 25 years or so, I was sitting at home with two babies under two years old, wondering how the heck I was going to balance my job in marketing with being a mum. Not least because pretty much all my clothes were by that time soiled with vomit or poo, and my brain was so addled from lack of sleep that I'd lost all confidence in my ability to achieve breakfast, let alone targets. So, I answered an advertisement by a local lady on the noticeboard at Morrisons, looking for five people to join her team doing sales and marketing, working from home, flexible hours, etc. But when she told me who she worked for, a well-known network marketing company, I immediately lost interest. In fact I never replied. I don't recall her name, and I'll bet she won't know mine, but it does make me smile to think how much I've changed and how I was so determined to be rude about her job. I do apologise.

Five years later, I'm lying in hospital having a lightbulb moment. Let me back-track a bit. I have a weird and rare form of arthritis. I have had it since I was 29, and right now it is under control with wonder drugs, but at the time I was on varying levels of steroids every day just to get out of bed. One well-meaning doctor decided to try me on a different drug, which went horribly wrong, and I reacted so badly I nearly died. But here's the crutch – I had known for *days* that I was in a bad way, but I did nothing about it because I was too busy trying to make my fledgling event management business a success. So, there I am, lying in hospital and wondering how I got there, and realising that I had actually nearly *killed* myself trying to do everything.

So, when I had recovered enough to get up, I told myself that I needed to *work less*, maybe *earn less*, but be there for my kids. It was then that network marketing walked back into my life, and literally saved my bacon.

My upline showed me how to talk to people about what the business does, how to book appointments and finally how to run them. She kept it really simple and made sure I could fit it in around my other commitments even on days when I'd had no sleep, was juggling my events business and my home admin, and my children were screaming at me over the Lego Movie. This truly was a business I could do on my terms.

So, I decided to give it a go, and the rest is history. But I still hate the term "network marketing"! I just can't help it, it's an ingrained reaction that is next to impossible to change. But you just have to accept that that is all it is and move on. After all, when a friend opens a local shop, is she accused of "selling to friends"? No, she is praised for her bravery and everyone tries to shop there for her. When someone you know starts a dog walking business and takes on friends as clients, is he accused of "selling to friends"? Of course not. When your cousin gets a job at the bank you use, is he expected to tell you to bank elsewhere? You get the gist; I won't go on. But these jobs are exactly the same as network marketing. We are all *always* connecting our business life with our personal life; we just might not have seen it that way before.

So, get used to the uncomfortable feeling and move on. After all, 20 million of us have a second income in the UK. Some might even be your friends selling to you!

Whatever you do, just stay in

A few months after starting my network marketing business, I attended a team day at Network HQ. My upline had gone to so much effort; she had planned the day meticulously, brought in some high-level speakers for us, even arranged a tour and put on a very nice free lunch. So, I thought, why not? It was the free lunch that did it.

Well, they say the people who go to the events do best in the network marketing business, and they are not wrong. This event was the turning point for me. Up until then, my scepticism was impacting my efforts. I'd only shown the business to a few people and had almost begrudgingly made it to my first promotion. It's fair to say I arrived at the company with a sense of trepidation. Would I be found out? Will everyone else here be super successful and wonder why I was even let in? And then one of the speakers stood up to give her presentation. She had the most beautiful piercing blue eyes that almost literally bore into me, and I sat up stock still. She started by saying:

"Make no mistake, this business is the best opportunity you will ever be given."

Her own confidence in her comment, her absolute 100% certainty that this was true, made my skin tingle. I listened, really listened. Her back story bore some resemblance to mine, but it wasn't this that made me stop and think; it was her faith in herself, and in the company. How many other employees of a large company would ever make a comment like that about their job? She finished her presentation with the following statement:

"No matter what else happens in your life, just stay in the business."

That was the lightbulb moment. I realised in that moment that network marketing was the kind of lifeline I'd been searching for. I was (and still am) a very busy woman – I was still running my event management company, had a mortgage as large as my two children were small, and was struggling with my health all the time. Plus, living far away from any family members, I had no help with any of it. So, I didn't need another boss to give me more work, or to add to the guilt when I felt I was failing at being a mum. I needed something that I could do *on my terms*. The idea that I could have a job that was there for me when I needed it and yet would take a back seat when I didn't was music to my ears.

Hello, Saviour Tortoise! That is network marketing for me. My business quietly chugs along in the background when I'm too busy to focus on it, but it is always there for me when I need it. So, here's the point: Never close your position. Always keep your options open. And, you never know, your upline might even grow a team underneath you. You are far more valuable to your upline than you'll ever be to a boss in a normal day job. Just stay in.

You and your choices

Why did you join the business?

It's obvious, right? You joined for the money! I mean, what a question! Of course you did. Except that you didn't.

Think about it. If you just joined for the money and nothing else, you'd have first asked for a pay rise or more hours in your current job – or even just got a normal job in the first place. But, if you've read this far already, I'd bet my bottom dollar that you did *not* join your network marketing business for the money. It was a factor, sure, but it's not the reason you joined.

Was it the holidays? The promotions? The car? Again, I'd bet not. Those things are nice to have, but again not *the* reason.

I'm asking you to really think about this because the real reason you joined the business dictates a lot about how you'll run with it. It will be the reason you decide on the number of hours you put in, the nature of the activities you'll choose to undertake and, moreover, it will impact how you manage your team and *their* reasons for joining. The single most important thing you can do is isolate your reason for joining because that will be what you keep coming back to when you're figuring out your way forward.

It won't be obvious. Ask anyone why they joined, and they'll immediately say it was for the money. But after half an hour of getting to know them, you'll realise it was way more than that. They were looking for *something to change*. So, how do you figure out what your something is? A good exercise I use all the time with my team is the "Why?" exercise. You start with the simple question:

Q: WHY do you need a second income?

A: To have more money, you donkey.

Q: Rude. But WHY is that important?

A: To be able to pay my divorce lawyer.

Q: Ah. And WHY is that important?

A: Because I don't want my kids to lose their home.

So, in this (very simplified but real) example, money was a factor but the real motivation for this gentleman was the desire to keep his children in the family home. That is huge, and much more motivating than money. OK yes, of course, some people's reasons will be immediate and sharp, like this one, while others may be less tangible or scary, but they are all valid nonetheless. For one partner in my team, his reason for joining the business was to find a focus again after losing his son to cancer. For another, she wanted to prove to herself that she was still worthy after being made redundant. And for another, she needed a job that would work around her dog she couldn't bear to rehome when her existing employer called her back to the office full-time.

For all of my partners, their reason for joining is personal, so it stands to reason that the way they run their own business is personal, too. The man with the legal fees to pay needed the income upfront and lots of it, whereas the person looking for a new focus was happy to grow his residual income slowly over time so that he could see his bank balance gradually increasing every month. Another partner in my team joined solely for the social aspect; she was feeling lonely and thrives on meeting new people. The lady needing a confidence boost after being made redundant found the training and personal development aspect of running a network marketing business the most rewarding thing. She doesn't do many appointments with customers, but she's now a respected author of self-help books!

And all of that is fine – network marketing caters for all of these people and more. For you to keep going, you need to figure out what you want to get out of the business because, I promise you, you will get out of it what you choose to put in.

Relax and keep it simple (you don't have to be perfect!)

I'm often asked why I don't work my network marketing business full-time when it pays so much better than my day job. The answer is because I want to keep the variety I have in my life. Frankly, network marketing wouldn't tax my brain enough because the role itself is *so simple*. But having two jobs and being a mum does make my life somewhat complicated, and I'm not alone.

So, for us to be successful at achieving our goals with network marketing, we need to do it the *relaxed* way. The high-achievers will hate me for saying this because they've achieved the big bucks by working hard, fast and furiously at their businesses. But that's not me (and I'm guessing it's not you either, otherwise you'd be reading a different book). I joined network marketing to get back my time to be with my kids, not spend more time working.

So, here's how (the big reveal):

The business is simple.

Keep it that way.

That's it!

To prove this to yourself, think about Andy Murray, one of Britain's most successful tennis players who won Wimbledon *twice*. I have never forgotten an interview with him on the BBC. (I'm not that old, but writing that sentence just made me feel positively wrinkly.) After his first victory, the interviewer asked Andy what had changed, after so many years of trying, to make him a champion. I think he was expecting an answer like "I got better coaching" or "well, I had to work harder". Andy replied, straight up, "I stopped trying." It blew my mind a little. By focusing on the basics, keeping it simple and just about the tennis, Andy had actually *relaxed into being a champion*. He focused on himself, did the job and got the result.

One of the best things about network marketing is anyone can do it. (It's also one of the *worst* things; I've met some absolute idiots, I can tell you!) But I won't take your money if I don't 100% believe you can do it, and I know you can because it's a simple system. Keep doing it and you'll get paid.

People who feel overwhelmed with network marketing – and I've been one of them – are feeling that way because they have fallen into the trap of overthinking it. They see the promotions, holiday points, bonuses, etc. and they think, "Oh god, I'm rubbish, everyone else is achieving these things but I'm not". Firstly, the reason your company offers these things is to keep people engaged. They come at an absolutely huge cost to the organisation, so there must be a lot of *un*-engaged people, people feeling just like you, who the company is trying to motivate. Secondly, these incentives are not the reason you joined. You joined to make money for a reason personal to you. Remember that reason. Just "do the do"; go through the actions and you'll get paid.

So, this is all very well, I hear you saying, *but I don't actually know how to do the role!*

I'll let you in on another secret: you don't have to know how to do the role!

I'm serious. Put yourself in the position of your customers. Who are you more likely to trust and believe: your old friend bumbling through a presentation about products and services *that they themselves use and trust,* laughing as you go along and enjoying a cuppa, or a slick salesperson giving you the chat-up lines you just know they've used on a thousand others before you? If you are using your organisation's product or service and truly believe that you are doing your mates a favour by showing it to them, your customers will come – without a shadow of a doubt. You don't need to be pitch-perfect in your presentation; in fact, it is better if you aren't. You are a human being, someone to be trusted because you are normal, you are a customer yourself, exactly like your customers.

I know it all sounds a bit scary. You'll be thinking, "Nah, come on, there's way more to it!" But really there isn't. Just make sure you do your first few appointments with your upline. You'll see it's very formulaic: you build rapport, you give the presentation, you and your customer decide if the business is right for them. You don't have to be right on point; all you have to do is *try*. "Do it wrong to get it right"; I heard another partner use this expression and I just had to borrow it because it is so true. Network marketing has to be *really* simple, otherwise the process can't be duplicated, and your upline will show you how to do it – don't be tempted to just go it alone. And if you don't like your upline (it happens!), there will be plenty of support to be found in other teams – head along to the local events to meet other local partners or distributors. Or get online and join your organisation's social media channels.

So, keep it simple, keep it natural and stop worrying about how to be perfect. You can be perfectly imperfect and still get away with it!

A little bit of effort goes a long way when you MOO

What does a day in the life of a network marketer actually look like? What are you meant to do? Well, this is your business, so you decide. There are so many ways to be successful – whatever success means to you – so do it your way. But if you have read thus far (thank you!) and you are wanting to get time back into your life for the fun stuff, you are definitely my kind of partner – the kind who wants to do well but, for whatever reason, has not got the headspace to throw all their energy behind it. So, let me tell you what works for me, and maybe it'll work for you or you can tweak it to suit you... your choice.

When I first started out with my business, I heard a ridiculously successful partner (the type who now earns hundreds of pounds every day before he wakes up) explain his Mode Of Operation (hilariously, his MOO). Every single day, on top of doing full-time jobs, he and his wife would not allow themselves to go to bed without having done one of the following three things that day: booked an appointment, signed up a new customer or taken on a new partner. Let's repeat that: *They wouldn't let themselves go to bed.*

Now, forgive me, but if you ever got into a career that didn't let you go to bed, I'd be telling you to give it up before you have a breakdown. Yes, this was their choice, and yes, it worked for them, but if my upline had told me to follow this MOO when I started out, I'd have run a mile! These guys were, and still are, hugely driven people and, don't get me wrong, I truly hope their business has delivered their dreams – my goodness, they deserve it – but, for most of us (especially those of us with young children), sleep is the pot of gold at the end of the rainbow. You never *ever* pass up the chance to sleep.

So, what do you do when you just want to have time for yourself and/or your family, but still need to make a bit more money than you're currently doing? Step in, Saviour Tortoise! You follow the relaxed – and yet terribly effective – MOO I created for me called the *Power of Three.*

The Power of Three is a MOO that takes up just three hours a week... *in total*! And you don't need a chunk of three hours in one go, in fact this fits into the nooks and crannies of your day. Arrived five minutes early to pick your kid up from football? Fab – five minutes clocked. Waiting for your dental appointment? Fab – twenty minutes clocked (or half an hour if it's *my* dentist). In fact, the only larger chunk of time you need in the Power of Three is one hour somewhere in your week (it can be one evening or at the weekend) in which to conduct an appointment. What's more, in these days of Zoom and Teams (or any other latest technological advancement designed to make our lives easier, even if we don't yet know how to unmute ourselves), you don't even need to factor in the time to travel to appointments either. Your appointment can be done whilst you're waiting for your takeaway to be delivered. Let me explain...

The Power of Three MOO:

1. One hour: For calling or texting the people on your list to book in two appointments for the following week. This time can be broken up into however many pieces to suit your busy lifestyle, so in fact you don't even notice you're clocking up that time.

2. Two hours: For the two appointments you booked in last week.

"Wait! Hang on," I can hear the eagle-eyed among you screaming, "you said only one paragraph ago that you only need one hour for actual appointments! I feel cheated!" And yes, dear reader, you are right, and herein lies the real beauty of this system. I said above that you need three hours *in total.* Rarely does it transpire that you actually need the full three hours because you can be guaranteed that at least one of the appointments you booked will subsequently call you to rearrange for the following week (if they are polite) or in fact not show up at all (if they are not). If they have rearranged... what amazing luck! You now only need to book one more appointment for the following week and your work is done! And if they didn't show up... wow, even better!

You've now got a whole hour free to make some more calls or texts, have a massage, read a book, chill...!

By following the Power of Three consistently, I promise you'll achieve at least one of these things:

1. A new customer a week – ker-ching!
2. A growing list of 'No For Now' people, which will make your appointments easier and even quicker down the line.
3. Thicker skin every time some 'friend' drops you in it.
4. Enough points to qualify for a free weekend break or whatever the promotion is at that time.
5. A new partner. Before you know it, three months have past and you've grown your team because someone has seen what you're doing, likes the look of it and thinks they can do the same – hello, new partner!

The important thing is to be just a little bit disciplined and stick to the plan. Do it consistently every week, the same as you would any other job. There will, of course, be times when you can't do it due to family emergencies or holidays, etc. but just get back to it as soon as you can. If you have worked at it consistently, you'll have grown a team that can step in for the times when you yourself can't work at your business. And even if you don't have a team yet and you need to take a step back, for whatever reason, use your upline to support you.

There are many MOOs in network marketing, my way is just one of them, and you'll find a way that suits you. The point is, you just need a good reason to do the business, a willingness to learn and, with the Power of Three, just three hours a week. Now get MOOing!

Recruit *unwillingly*

Recruiting.

The word alone makes me shudder. It makes me remember awful job interviews where you have to give cringe-worthy answers to questions like "If you were an animal, what would you be?" Well, as you know by now, in my head I'm a tortoise, but I couldn't exactly give that answer in a job interview! In network marketing, though, recruiting is worse, oh way worse than that. You are recruiting *friends*, not colleagues! Uuuurgh! I feel dirty just thinking about it.

So, when I expressed this sentiment to my upline at the start of my journey with network marketing, I feared I'd get the cold shoulder. After all, we are meant to be recruiting everyone from our auntie to the postie, right? What use to you is a new partner who doesn't want to recruit? It's like hitting the jackpot and then being told you have to burn the money!

My upline threw me a bone – odd for a tortoise, so let's go with a piece of lettuce. He said, and I quote...

"You don't have to grow a team."

There. That was it. It blew my tiny little mind – What?

I don't have to recruit? I can do this business my way? I thought recruiting was the whole point of network marketing! "Nope", said he, "you can just look for customers if that's what you want. But you will find..."

At this moment I scoffed a little, thinking *here we go, I knew it was too good to be true...*

"...you will find that the more people you show this business to, the more people will want to do what you do and you will recruit unwillingly."

Recruit *unwillingly*. What a weird concept. But he wasn't wrong. I'd gathered over 50 customers before I recruited my first partner, and even then I tried to talk said 'gullible partner' person out of it. But my new partner was adamant, he wanted a slice of the pie, and who was I to argue? So, back on the phone I got to my upline: "I've become an unwilling recruiter. I've got a partner. Darn it! Now what do I do?"

"That's brilliant!" he said (bless him). "If you don't feel ready to train him, I can do that, you'll still get all the benefits of having him in your team." That was the moment when it hit me that the team works. You don't *have* to be a leader, you don't *have* to be driven, you don't in fact *have* to be that good at anything, because the more time you spend in the business, the more you realise that there is always someone in your upline or downline who can fill in your blanks. People ask me all the time how I recruit. The truth is that I don't. I don't go looking for partners. That's probably why I'm still just a few rungs up the ladder but, you know what, I'm happy with that! This way I get to work only with people I actually want to work with. Who can say that about their office job?

As it turned out, my new partner was a bit of a dream to work with. He diligently did his training, booked appointments, even recruited a few partners. He has since gone very quietly about his business. He is a classic example of the kind of person I want in my team – self-sufficient and just 'doing the do' when he has time. He could do so much more with the business, but it is his choice not to and I respect that. It is people like him who are the bread and butter of network marketing. We are not all ambitious superstars, so it stands to reason that we are also not failures when we have to put our businesses down for a while. We all need quiet partners in our teams, and I'm forever grateful that my partner didn't listen to me when I begged him not to sign up!

I've carried on being an unwilling recruiter. I still go into appointments with the mindset that I'm there to help my customers, not necessarily to recruit them. I also don't show the business to everyone as we are taught to (naughty of me, I know). Frankly, while I know I need people in my team to really make my business take off financially, I'm not interested in taking people's money off them as a joining fee unless I'm sure they are somebody I'd want to work with. That doesn't necessarily mean they have to be the next starlet who'll fly up the food chain; quite the opposite, in fact. It just means I like to recognise a little bit of me in them – someone who doesn't need constant prodding to do the job, someone who is willing to learn and someone who has a reason to make a change in their lives. I'm not their mother or their torturer, I'm their colleague, and we work together towards their goal, whatever that might be.

As time has gone on and my belief in the positive changes this business can bring to people's lives has grown, the more willing I have become to share the pie, and I've found myself actually enjoying supporting others. So, if you are an unwilling recruiter, who vomits at the mere suggestion of recruiting, please just carry on.

And so, to summarise...

You might have noticed that I have a real tendency to choose the path of least resistance. Frankly, it's a miracle I became a network marketer in the first place, and it's certainly not a role I've ever felt comfortable with. So, why do I still do it? Because I've found a way to truly suck at network marketing and yet still do rather well, thank you very much.

My network marketing business has been my Saviour Tortoise in so many ways. Yes, the financial benefits can't be underestimated; when COVID closed my events business and made me a home-schooler, it helped pay the bills. But it's more than that. Having my business under my arm has made me less stressed as a person, and that's improved my health no end. Having my business meant I could cut my hours in my job and spend more time with my children. I can watch their sports days; I can go to their nativities. This is time with them that's incredibly precious to me, and I've been able to be present for them.

Yes, you know all of this; you might have watched the videos. But there's one hidden benefit that is right up there with the rest. By following the Power of Three, doing my MOO if you will, I managed to take my family to Florida. Sitting on that plane, getting ready to take off, watching the kids' excitement at the prospect of seeing (I want to say Mickey Mouse but actually it was) Bumblebee, I had such an enormous sense of achievement. I'd made this mad idea work for me. I'd put on my big girl's pants and run with it. This was *my* doing. *I did this.*

I was so proud of myself, and this is the *truest* benefit of network marketing. What you get with network marketing that you don't often get elsewhere is enormous personal development and recognition. Get ready to feel good about yourself. You don't need to run hard and fast, you can walk in your comfy slippers if you like, but make the commitment to yourself that you will do it - you'll find out what you are truly capable of.

I can promise you this – it'll be much more than you ever thought possible.

Printed in Great Britain
by Amazon

52409862R00025